Chaos to Calmish

Diary of a Pesky Puppy's first year

This book is dedicated to my wonderful
husband, our two daughters, and to my
assistants Gareth and Catherine. With huge
thanks to you all for putting up with me.

Also by Carol Clark:

Pesky Puppy to Perfect Pet

Foreword

A new puppy. A cuddly, warm, baby-smelling bundle of joy. A wonderful, happy, exciting event. But it's not all roses and champagne. Trying to manage your wriggling worm while you're both covered in poo is disgusting. Your pup chewing through the phone wire while you're on the phone is exasperating. Concentrating on writing that urgent email while your pup is barking at shadows is downright impossible.

Having a new puppy is a fantastic, happy, scary, frustrating, exciting, amusing, annoying time that will change your life upside down.

You'll get lots of advice from everyone you meet. All well-meaning and all different. You'll have devoured loads of books about how to raise a puppy. Some you found yourself and some recommended by friends. But the often conflicting advice can leave you more confused than ever...

I explain what to do about all the usual puppy problems you'll face in my own book, *Pesky Puppy to Perfect Pet*. It also includes all the basic training you need to raise a great family pet. It's available in paperback or Kindle version on Amazon.

But it doesn't help you "in the moment" as it were. We all wrestle with the reality. It's nice to have great information to hand. But it doesn't always help with some of the problems you'll be wrestling with, such as when to move your pup's crate out of the bedroom, or how to clean runny poo off your sheepskin rug, or whether that plant your puppy has just chewed to bits is poisonous or not.

You'll have great plans to train your puppy right from the start - but life can take over. When we got Gus, I'd recently started running my dog training business. But I was also doing some regular management consultancy work away in England for several days at a time, followed by needing to write up reports. Not ideal, but pretty typical - there is rarely an ideal time to get a dog.

I'd always planned to keep a diary of my new puppy's progress and what we did. I wanted to keep a good record of who he met and what we did so I could chart his progress for the first year. As always, good intentions didn't last. The later entries are far sparser than I had intended. But I hope you find it interesting to read about how I struggled at times, despite having had four previous puppies and despite having taught dog club training classes for around fifteen years and run my own training business for two years.

This short book is the honest, contemporaneous diary of the first year of Gus's life (2012-2013). The aim is to show, warts and all, what life with a new puppy is like. Reading it back now, there are many things I would have changed. Hindsight is always a wonderful thing. I've added notes in boxes after some sections to say what I could have done better. And to note where I made mistakes.

Life with a new puppy is day to day chaos. I hope this book helps you realise that you can eventually achieve calm - or at least calmish.

Carol Clark
KCAI (CD* Beh), ADipCBM
Dog Trainer and Behaviourist

TABLE OF CONTENTS

Chaos to Calmish: A puppy diary

Introducing Gus

September 5th 2012

Five minutes in my arms and Gus had stolen my heart. I had no choice. Ignoring the little voice in my head that said take your time, think about this more, I decided there and then to bring him home.

Gus came from a farm near Kilcoo in County Down, Northern Ireland, after our daughter saw an ad on Gumtree. He was born after an accidental mating between the farm's ten-month-old collie bitch and a neighbour's four year-old working sheepdog. There were seven pups in the litter. The mum, who was quite wary of approaching us, was very thin and scrawny looking. The farmer said she'd lost a lot of weight while feeding the pups.

Gus was outside in a large pen with his brothers and sisters in one corner of a field. The farm was in a very quiet location and had a wonderful view of the nearby loch. The pups had the run of the field each day, alongside some sheep. They were shut in the pen at night. The teenage daughter of the family did most of the care of the puppies, giving them cuddles and feeding them. They had been wormed but not vaccinated.

The pups had not been in the house and they'd only seen the family and two farm workers. The farmer wasn't even sure exactly which date they'd been born, so we calculated Friday 13th July. (He was sure it was a Friday and knew they were around 8 weeks old.)

Was that date an omen? Time would tell.

LESSONS I LEARNED:

Gumtree is not the best place to look for a puppy!

We'd lost our previous dog under difficult circumstances in June 2012 and I wanted (needed?) another dog to fill that yawning chasm of unhappiness. That day, we'd been down to Dublin to see a litter but the puppies weren't what I wanted. I'd seen another litter of pups but they weren't going to be available for a few more weeks. I was feeling down and the rest of the family were pressing for a new puppy as soon as possible.

Farm bred collies have strong herding instincts and need for work. I had some reservations about getting one. But once I'd cuddled that lovely warm

---

puppy for a bit, my husband started negotiating to buy him there and then.

Always try to visit a puppy at least twice during their first few weeks to give yourself time to decide if that particular puppy is really right for you. Try and make your decision with your head, not your heart. But I know it's really difficult. I didn't follow my own advice with Gus!

Puppies are best raised in a house environment, which gives them the best start in life. They get used to all the household noises, smells and activities right from the start. The best breeders choose the mum and dad carefully to try to make sure that the puppies have a great temperament, too. You can usually get a good idea of how the pups are going to turn out from meeting their mum (and their dad, if possible).

Despite knowing all this, I still took Gus.

Puppy Diary

Dog: Gus

Breed: Border Collie

Colour: Black and white

Age: 7 weeks 5 days   DOB 13/7/12

Each day I'm going to write down what we did and what happened. I want to keep a diary to help me keep a record of who Gus met and what he experienced - his socialisation.

(Socialisation is about helping puppies, and older rescue dogs, learn about all the different people, animals, places, and things they will need to know about, meet and cope with in life.)

Eat, Pee and Poo: The First Week

Day 0: 5/9/12

Gus came home this evening in a cardboard box on my knee in the front seat. He was sick 4 times during the journey. I was so glad I had a whole roll of kitchen towel in the boot. The cardboard box protected my clothes (mainly). A little sick goes a long, long way. And the smell, well. Gus coped well with the short, noisy, ferry journey from Strangford to Portaferry, then the final nine mile car journey was mercifully sick-free. Though the smell remained…

When we got home, we carried Gus round to our back door. He explored the yard and did his first tiddle - hurrah. Then Gus came into the house. It was the first time he'd experienced a house, but he was happy to wander round and explore. He kept close by us all the time. It's too easy to step on or trip over that tiny bundle of fluff, so we'll have to be careful.

I took Gus out to the yard every hour but it was only on the third occasion he finally pee'd again. I think he might have been dehydrated from the sickness. No pee or poo accidents in the house -

yet! Later that evening I carried him out with me to meet a client and her dog. Gus is so tiny and cuddly at least it's easy to carry him around, but that won't last long I'm sure.

Gus showed a little interest in playing with his first toy, a rag rope, but really he just wanted to chew it. He seemed to enjoy the television and watched it quite a bit. He ate some supper and drank some water. He slept a lot this evening, unsurprisingly.

We decided to put him in a crate downstairs in my study for the night – big mistake! Gus went into the crate quite happily at first. But then he howled almost continuously for six hours, even though I mainly stayed close by the crate, huddled in a blanket. He stopped howling only four times for between 10-20 mins. I tried to creep upstairs to bed each time, but instead I was up and down the stairs like a yo-yo all night. No sleep. Knackering.

We desperately need another option for tomorrow night.

MET: Our family (3 adults: David, me and our adult daughter Tricia); One of my clients (adult) and her dog, a Shih Tzu X

EXPERIENCES: Car travel; Ferry travel; Courtyard (surfaces: paving, gravel); House – 4 rooms: various flooring (tiles, mats, concrete); Television; First toy (rag dumbbell)

LESSONS I LEARNED: I should have immediately taken him out of his crate this first night, but we did not have anything else to hand. Mea culpa. We were not properly prepared - I remember having to ring Tricia on our way home to get her to do an emergency dash to the pet shop for food! Luckily, having had dogs before, we did have most of the other stuff we needed.

It would, of course, have been much better to take our time and make a more considered purchase. That would have given us more time to plan things better and make sure we had everything ready for when the new puppy came home. I've written a free advice sheet on *Preparing for a new puppy or dog*, available from our website, www.downdog.co.uk so you don't make the mistakes I did!

Day 1: 6/9/12

I'd forgotten just how much time it takes to look after a new puppy. You can't do anything else because you have to take him out so often and you need to watch him constantly to make sure he's not peeing or pooing or chewing something he shouldn't. It's hard work.

Gus and I both struggled to keep our eyes open today, after an extremely broken nights sleep for both of us.

Amazingly he hadn't pee'd or poo'd in the crate - though he was more than ready to tiddle as soon as we got outside. Had no toilet accidents in the house all day. I took him outside every hour on the dot. He poo'd twice today – a little loose, but OK.

Gus had his collar fitted this morning. He scratched at it quite a few times but by lunchtime he seemed to have forgotten about it. This afternoon I clipped the lead to his collar and attached the handle end to me round a belt, so it was like an umbilical cord. Gus objected at first and had a short fight against it. But soon he accepted it quite well and we wandered around the house with him following me happily.

He was happy to go into the crate of his own free will when I was standing right by it, but I didn't even try to shut the door. I hope he hasn't got too many bad associations with it after last night.

Gus had several other new experiences today. He met the postman and another delivery man and had a short play on our lawn.

He follows me everywhere and even gets distressed if I go to the toilet. It's like having a tiny, fluffy shadow.

Gus got lots of treats (pieces of his dry complete dog food) today whenever he paid any attention to me.

He loves being touched all over. And I love having those soft, squidgy puppy cuddles. He seems to enjoy having his ears fondled, he didn't object to me gently opening his mouth and he happily let me pick up and feel his feet and toes.

He is eating well. He dives straight into his bowl and rather bolts his food actually. We'll need to monitor this as it's not good for dogs to bolt food.

Gus went to sleep on his soft bed in a cardboard box right by my bed tonight. We both need sleep.

MET: Postman and Delivery driver

EXPERIENCED: House – wooden floor; Collar and lead – also following me on lead; Grass; More toys

LESSONS I LEARNED: Fitting a collar and lead early on lets your puppy get used to them before you use them to take him for walks. It also makes it easy to take him out regularly (oh, so, so regularly) for toilet breaks. An umbilical lead (one end attached to the puppy and the other end attached to you round a belt) can be really useful as it keeps the puppy close, so you are more likely to notice what he's doing and can quickly stop things you don't want him to do. At least I was sensible that night and put Gus in a box by my bed. I should have done that right from the start.

Day 2: 7/9/12 - 8 weeks old

What a change! Gus slept through for nearly 7 hours. Bliss! So did I. We were both shattered.

Gus went straight out for his tiddle (a very big tiddle) when he woke up. He also had a big poo. Another day with no accidents in the house. He is doing brilliantly, though of course we are watching him like a hawk and taking him out very regularly every hour, also when he wakes up after a sleep, after play sessions and any other time we think he needs it. Good job the weather's fairly good this week.

Gus saw the vacuum cleaner for the first time. He was a bit wary of it at first, and kept his distance, but he coped with me vacuuming. He just sat and watched.

Gus came for the short car journey to the vets in a box on my knee. He wasn't sick again thank goodness, but it was only a mile. He was happy to meet all the new people, and he was quite content with the vet examining him. He had his first vaccination. He didn't even seem to notice the needle, as I made sure he had his face in a box of food at the time. He will be microchipped at his next visit at around 11 weeks of age. We wormed him today too.

He follows me everywhere. I have to be so careful not to fall over him or step on him. It needs constant surveillance and it's really tiring.

Gus gets lots of rewards and treats (kibble) when he sits politely. He's now sitting for anything and everything – he's quickly cottoned onto this. I think he's quite bright.

We bought him an anti-gobble bowl today (one of the bowls with big knobbles built into the base) to stop him bolting his food – it seems to be working well.

He came (carried) into our training arena with me. I put him down for a short explore so he could experience sand.

Several of our friends came around to see him. There's nothing more attractive than a cuddly, wriggly new puppy! Gus saw a total of 10 new people today, which was excellent. The more the better, as long as they take their shoes off and wash their hands. He also saw some cars, a trailer and a mini-digger coming off a trailer; and then it noisily working in the garden to dig holes.

I think I'm as exhausted as he is this evening. We went to bed early and he dropped off to sleep very quickly with me dangling my hand into the box touching him gently. Reassuring for both of us.

MET: Vet and reception staff plus two other people there; Three adult friends and an 8 year-old boy; Two builders (adults)

EXPERIENCED: Sand surface; car travel again; cars, trailer; Mini-digger working; men shovelling concrete; Vacuum cleaner

LESSONS I LEARNED: Bolting food can be dangerous because it might cause bloat, which needs urgent attention from a vet. A feeding bowl with knobbles, or putting an object such as a plastic yoghurt pot or a large stone upside down in the bowl can help because it forces the puppy to eat smaller mouthfuls at a time.

Day 3: 8/9/12

It feels like Gus has been here forever, not just three days.

Gus woke me by whining at 5.30am. Not a bad night's sleep though. I took him out for his tiddle then we came back to bed and he went back to sleep for another hour. I just dozed, listening to his puppy snuffles and squeaks.

It was another busy day for both of us. Gus came out on his lead with me down the garden to help me feed and clean out the hens. Very exciting, hens! He was grabbing and tearing at the wire with his teeth and paws, trying to get at them. Eventually he gave up, sat quietly and watched them.

After breakfast I carried him out to meet the owners at our puppy class (including a ten-year-old child). Gus saw the other dogs from my arms, then he stayed inside with David until our next class when he came out (carried again) and met some new owners and two friendly adult dogs. I decided to put him down on the sand. It's our private arena so safe enough. He immediately shot under my chair, but by the end of the lesson he went voluntarily and happily up to both the dogs to say hello. I was delighted with him.

Gus stayed indoors with Tricia after lunch. They practised fun recalls and played with tug toys. At tea time he met my mum and dad for the first time. Gus snuggled up to dad who doesn't like dogs, but was rather taken with him. Overall Gus behaved beautifully.

Gus likes hide chews and will lie down for some time gnawing at them. The anti-gobble bowl is working well. Gus sits without being asked for his food to be put down, though he dives in as soon as it hits the floor. And he has decided for himself to sit to ask us for attention, which he does regularly.

Gus actually stayed in the kitchen sleeping whilst I was in my study - a small sign of progress in his independence. Perhaps I'll be able to get some work done this week after all.

He seems to cope fairly well with loud noises but he barks when he hears certain noises such as me moving my computer mouse wheel and stirring a metal pan with a wooden spoon. Wonder why these in particular?

Gus played more with his toys with us this evening. I rolled a ball around. He enjoyed running after it and even tried to bring it back once or twice. Then I gently introduced a brush. Gus was happy to let me brush his back and sides and didn't chew it too much.

We went to bed at 11pm and he went to sleep within a few minutes with me just gently touching him. It's soothing for both of us.

The end of another busy day.

MET: Mum and dad; 3 strange(!) men; 5 strange women; 1 child aged 10; 3 puppies seen; 2 friendly adult dogs interaction

EXPERIENCED: In sand arena with other dogs and people; Hens; Tennis ball

LESSONS I LEARNED: You'll find many vets warn against taking your puppy out anywhere until they have completed their vaccinations. But it's absolutely fine to *carry* your puppy out and about and take them in the car. I should have taken more notice of his reactions to noises. It later became a problem, as you'll see.

Day 4: 9/9/12

It's hard work and very tiring having to watch Gus all the time. I love having all the puppy cuddles and it's fascinating watching him learn about the world, but it's almost worse than having a baby. There's just no time to do anything else.

Gus slept well again in his box by my bed. He is SO good. And SO cuddly - I just love stroking that soft puppy fur.

He still hasn't had any accidents in the house. He went to the back door three times today when he wanted to go out. I'm still taking him out every hour of course. He's claimed the flowerbeds as his pee and poo areas which we are very happy with. Interestingly, he seems to prefer to hide from us watching while performing. Don't blame him, but we will have to watch he doesn't do that in the house.

Gus came out with me first thing to help feed, move and clean out the hens and then he pottered around the sand arena whilst we set the agility equipment up for our class. Gus had great fun exploring, walking on and climbing on things. He went through the tunnel of his own volition and also decided to walk over the seesaw with me letting it down VERY gently.

He has stopped fighting against the lead and is walking quite well on it. He watched the mini-digger being reloaded onto the truck and driven away.

Gus saw and heard the washing machine and tumble dryer being loaded and turned on with no problems. In fact, he decided the pile of dirty washing was a good bed. But the steam iron surprised him initially - he leapt backwards when it spat and hissed. I have to admit I laughed. He seems quite sound curious/sound sensitive with some noises.

Gus enjoys playing with his toys. He played on his own with the tyre ring for a while but I interrupted him so we could play together. He takes his toys into his crate happily and voluntarily, so I'm glad he's not associated the crate with bad emotions after that dreadful first night.

He had some diarrhoea this evening, (outside, thank goodness). Luckily he produced it on the flowerbed, so I just hosed it away. It was very watery but he seems well enough otherwise. Thank goodness the mess wasn't in the house, I dread to think how I would have cleaned it up.

Could it be the change of food or possibly the vaccination or wormer? Not sure. Possibly both? Will see how he is tomorrow.

Gus is learning about not using teeth on human skin. He responds well to "ow" and he's being very gentle most of the time except when he has his short, mad 'zoomie' fits, which happen early most evenings. He does bite a bit more then. Saying "ow" to interrupt him then praising him for not biting works sometimes, but not always. Chew toys are also proving useful when he's in a bitey mood. Typical puppy.

MET: Adult man again

EXPERIENCED: Digger again; agility equipment; Washing machine and tumble dryer; Ironing board and steam iron (admittedly a rarity in this house!)

LESSONS I LEARNED: How tiring it is having a new puppy! The biting is especially annoying, but totally normal. All puppies bite as it's part of the way they learn about the world.

'Zoomie' fits are totally normal too - where the puppy just runs around madly, with tail tucked in, for half an hour or so, usually early evening - when they can be especially bitey, so it's best to be prepared with something your puppy enjoys chewing.

Day 5: 10/9/12

How quickly puppies grow up. We're already seeing so much change in Gus.

Gus woke me at 6.30 this morning. I can live with this!

After he'd had a tiddle outside, I let him explore our bedroom while I got dressed. He found the waste paper bin and stole a paper tissue – I think he will be another tissue stealer like our previous dog, as Gus tried to run away with it when I went to take it from him. We will need to remember to put tissues only in closed bins in future. After a sharp interrupt noise from me when he went back towards the bin he stayed well away from it.

He walked beautifully on lead when going out to do the hens and fill the bird feeders.

Gus still tries to gobble his food. I am practising feeding drills: putting a little food into his bowl then petting him while he eats it, adding more food then petting him again. It's working well. He looks up and wags his tail most times, though he still tries to eat too quickly. But the anti-gobble knobbly bowl is working quite well.

Today Gus brought me one of his toys when he

wanted to play. So sweet! He's beginning to learn fetch – he enjoys chasing a rolling ball and most times he will bring it back. He also enjoys tug-of-war games and, of course, he loves chewing. Playing with toys means he's not trying to bite us as much, so we encourage lots of toy play.

Gus met the shopping delivery driver this afternoon then David took care of Gus while I put the shopping away.

Then - horrors! I found a dried tiddle accident in the front sitting room behind the sofa. It was probably a couple of days old (Saturday? First day he was in there) – the first and only accident so far.

Vicky, our other daughter, arrived home mid-afternoon. In all the melee of unloading her car we took our eyes off Gus for a moment and he grabbed the 5 foot-high umbrella fern in the hall and pulled it over – what a mess! Took a while to clear it all up. The fern will never be the same again.

Otherwise Gus has been very good. He's looking up at me a lot and he runs to us happily when we call him. He is now much braver, staying where he's dozing if I go out of the room. Twice he's chosen to wander off to a quiet corner to snooze. I keep practising going in and out of the room briefly when he is calm and tired.

What a difference a day or so makes! Gus is gaining some independence.

MET: Vicky: mum & dad again; the Tesco delivery driver

EXPERIENCED: Shopping delivery; Washing machine and tumble dryer again

---

LESSONS I LEARNED: Some dogs love to steal and eat paper tissues - three of my previous dogs have enjoyed it. Luckily tissues are safe for puppies to eat. Puppies who run away with things can be showing early signs of a tendency to resource guard, that is, the puppy wants to protect things he sees as valuable. Gus has got that tendency - see the diary entry for day 27 where it showed itself again. Five days with no pees or poos in the house was pretty good but inevitably it was going to happen!

Day 6: 11/9/12

I'm shattered. I've forgotten just how time-consuming, tiring and frustrating having a small puppy is.

Not such a good start today. Gus woke around 7am and I took him straight outside for a tiddle as usual. But while I was getting dressed Gus poo'd on the mat in David's study. Why do they always choose a furry mat? It's so difficult to get it clean. I'd forgotten just how unpleasant it is cleaning up poo, even when it's formed. The downside of having a puppy. It also demonstrates the downside of Gus gaining some independence and wandering off instead of staying close to me.

Gus came out with me to feed the hens and birds then I did some more practice with touching him while he was eating – all going well.

He ran off when I started to use our small dustette. He doesn't seem to like loud noises. I forget so many things are new to him then I'm stupidly surprised when he reacts to something like our dustette.

Gus travelled in a box on the front seat of the car into Kircubbin. I carried him along the street to meet people and see traffic. It all went very well. No problems (sickness) in the car. When I carried him down the street, he was slightly scared by a minibus, but seemed fine with all other traffic, just looking around and pricking up his ears at everything new. He met loads of new people, including five babies/toddlers in prams, two men, my craft group ladies and a security guard in a helmet and carrying a bank box – excellent!

Gus is happily going off to sleep at a little distance from me now, though still in the same area.

Unfortunately we had two pee accidents in my study today – one drying one from last night which I hadn't noticed until today (bad mummy) and one this morning which I half interrupted. It was my fault as I didn't take him out straight away as soon as he woke up. He also had a pee accident in the kitchen this evening when I was out. Rats! That's four today. Need to up the surveillance – I will go back to the umbilical cord lead now he's getting bold enough to wander off on his own more.

He met a teenage pupil of Tricia's this evening when she came for a lesson.

Gus was quite hyper all afternoon and evening.

He didn't settle much and was on the go all the time, running about, grabbing things, biting a LOT, having odd surreptitious chews at the furniture and stealing my slippers. Very tiring. We will monitor this – perhaps the current food is too high in protein (31%)? Or perhaps he's just finding his feet. He's certainly finding his teeth...but giving him a toy to tug/chew instead of him chewing us works quite well.

MET: 5 babies/toddlers in prams and their 2 mums; two men; craft group ladies; A security guard in a helmet and carrying a bank box; a teenager

EXPERIENCED: Kircubbin traffic; Car travel again; Dustette

LESSONS I LEARNED: It is very tiring caring for a new puppy. You want to do everything right but it's inevitable there will be problems; pee and poo accidents, things being chewed, and biting - lots of biting.

Oh, and I still haven't found out how best to clean furry mats.

Day 7: 12/9/12

It's never too early to start some basic training.

Gus was tired last night, unsurprisingly. He slept from 11 pm until 7.20am.

No pee or poo accidents today. I successfully interrupted one attempt in the sitting room.

Gus is definitely finding his feet and getting much braver. He's now happy to wander off round the house on his own and to wander all round the yard. He's been very active again today.

I vacuumed again today and he ran away from the vacuum cleaner when I turned it on, so I will need to do some training to help him cope with that. Also he ran out of the room when I played a few notes on the piano, so that's another thing he doesn't like. Everything he doesn't like is noise related. I think he might be very sound sensitive. He goes out of the room when I turn the washing machine and tumble dryer on, too.

Gus now plays nicely with toys and us and he happily runs up to greet all our visitors.

He goes into his crate very happily, but he gets stressed if I try to shut the crate door. But if I only close it very briefly (1-2 seconds) he is OK. So that's yet another thing that needs practice. I need more time - it all takes so much time.

He's a clever dog. He is learning 'sit' and 'down' and does them when we ask him to most times. He sits very nicely of his own accord when he wants attention or food or whatever. It's taking him longer to learn 'down', though he does it easily when I use a food lure.

Another great benefit of doing lots of tiny bits of training is that he can't be getting into mischief, chewing and biting.

MET: Postman again; adult female friend

EXPERIENCED: Vacuum cleaner; washing machine and tumble dryer (again)

LESSONS I LEARNED: Don't plan to do anything other than look after your puppy for the first few days. You'll be in and out from the garden like a yo-yo, feeding small meals every few hours, stopping him chewing your shoes and trying to stop him biting you by giving him lots of toys instead. But you'll also have fun playing with him, cuddling him and just watching him exploring all the new things he'll find in this exciting world you've brought him to.

Rattles, Bangs and Squeaks: The Second Week

Day 8: 13/9/12

Gus has been part of our family for a whole week already. How time flies. I can't imagine life without him now.

I'd forgotten how much time you spend obsessing about your puppy's bodily functions, especially about <u>where</u> they occur! Dealing with the biting and chewing can be very wearing too, but the gorgeous, heart-warming cuddles make up for a lot.

Today was another busy day with, happily, no pee or poo accidents.

After breakfast, Gus came in his box in the car with us to Ballyhalbert harbour where I carried him to watch six NI Water workers putting together the outflow for the new works. Four men wore hard hats and overalls, two were in waders, so they all looked new and different types of people to a tiny puppy.

Gus also saw a launch out in the water, a large fishing boat moored in the harbour and the sea itself (it was very calm today). He was frightened by the noise of the generator the workers were using (it was very loud, to be fair) and he was also scared by the noise of a hand electric drill initially, but he settled quietly in my arms fairly quickly. I was pleased how well he travelled in the car, he seems much happier about car travel now. No more sickness.

Gus also met the postman again, a new delivery driver and the BT man who came to fix our internet. Nine new people today. Good.

This evening, Tricia got out a new squeaky toy. Unexpectedly Gus was really wary of it. So we just left it lying on the floor. After a short while Gus came to sniff it, but he didn't want to play with it. I thought ALL dogs loved squeaky toys. Gus is obviously special! We will need to work hard on getting him used to lots of different noises, clearly. He is definitely a noise sensitive dog.

Even after a whole week with us, we are still finding out new things about Gus.

MET: Six NI Water workers; hard hats, overalls, waders; Delivery man; postman (again); BT engineer

EXPERIENCED: Generator; Electric drill;

Sea and boats

LESSONS I LEARNED: Meeting lots of new people of all different types and ages is the most important part of socialisation. I'm quite proud of how well we did with Gus. Keeping this diary helped remind me that I needed to find new things and people for Gus to see and meet each day if possible.

Day 9: 14/9/12– 9 weeks old

Gus is growing up so quickly. We are getting into some sort of routine, finally, and Gus is settling in to our family well.

He had a quieter day today to celebrate his nine-week milestone.

Today was a day for consolidating what has been learnt so far. Gus was quite sleepy most of the day. He was catching up I think - he has been growing very rapidly, which is obvious when I'm carrying him. I wonder how long I can keep doing that?

Gus is learning to 'sit' and 'down' well, so today we added 'stand'. We do several short (2-5 minute) little sessions each day doing bits of training, which makes him think and also has the great benefit of tiring him out.

Gus loves playing with toys, which is great, because if he's chewing and biting toys he's not chewing and biting us. He enjoys retrieving a ball, but he's far less interested in bringing back other types of toy if I throw them.

Unfortunately he had two pee accidents today. I caught one mid-stream, but missed the second. Naughty mummy. As I was cleaning up the second pee he started chewing a chair leg. I interrupted him before he could do too much damage.

A microlight flew over the house this afternoon. Gus barked at it and tried to chase after it. I've noticed he seems very interested in watching planes - we have a lot that fly over us, both small planes from Newtownards airfield and jets coming and going from Belfast City airport.

Gus persisted in trying to get at my dinner this evening (carry-out kebab and chips) which I was eating on the settee in front of the TV. Trying to control a wriggly, squirming puppy determined to push himself up onto my lap while I'm trying to keep my fork and plate away from him and not spill anything was quite funny actually. He obviously doesn't make healthy food choices. But I must teach him some food manners and train him to 'leave' my food alone.

Gus has new sleeping arrangements from today. I moved his bed from the cardboard box, which he's now outgrown, into a crate by my bed. He went straight in, was not worried by the door being closed (as I was lying right next to him) and he fell asleep within minutes.

MET: Postman yet again

EXPERIENCED: Low flying small plane/microlight; Crate for sleeping

LESSONS I LEARNED: To take more notice of the odd behaviours Gus showed! I wish now I had taken more notice of his reactions to noises and to planes. You'll see later on in this diary that those two things have become the main ongoing problems. I should have done more to help him be more confident with noises and taught him to ignore planes at this stage in his short life.

Day 10: 15/9/12

Busy Saturday with me running my dog training classes.

Gus had a busy day. I carried him out to join half the puppy class and then he stayed out with me for the whole adult class. He met three new dogs: beagle and westie puppies and a grown springer spaniel. Initially Gus backed away, but within less than a minute he was happy to interact with them. He enjoyed meeting the big dogs he met last week. He showed off the basic training we have done so far. One client gave him a teething ring type toy which has become his new favourite.

Then this afternoon he watched the flyball session and met Tricia's friend Gina and her lovely cross breed dog Jess.

He was tired this evening and had a slight tantrum when prevented from doing what he wanted, which was to chew my slippers. He pulled away from me then bit, whined and growled a bit, but he soon settled.

Gus is getting good at telling David when he wants some dinner – by running to where the bag of food is and sitting staring at it! That doesn't necessarily work with me and Tricia though. We're made of sterner stuff. Like all puppies Gus would eat all day if he could. He has to learn to wait for mealtimes.

Gus slept a lot this evening. It was a very tiring day meeting all those new people and dogs.

MET: Class attendees; young adult female and her cross breed dog; Several different new breeds of dogs and puppies

EXPERIENCED: Rally and flyball; Vacuum cleaner again

Day 11: 16/9/12

It's still taking so much of my time and focus looking after this gorgeous but demanding puppy. But I feel we are getting into a workable routine now.

Gus met five new dogs and 6 new people in the agility class today.

He was very happy to meet people as usual. He was a little wary of the dogs at first, but if given time to settle, he was then happy to meet and greet them. I tried tying him up to the fence while we set out the course, but he whined and yapped. As soon as he was untied, he watched happily.

Gus adventurously climbed up the A frame - but he was too scared to come down again so I had to lift him down. One client cuddled him for a while. Suddenly I noticed that he had his head in her tum bag eating her dog's sausages! Cheeky puppy.

Later, he moved away when I picked up the dustette then used it - that noisy thing again! We laid and lit the stove fire today - autumn is coming - but he wasn't bothered by that at all, even though the procedure can be quite noisy and the stove doors squeak quite loudly.

No accidents again today.

MET: 5 new dogs; 6 new people including two teenagers

EXPERIENCED: Agility; Dustette again; Laying and lighting the stove fire

Day 12: 17/9/12

I was out a lot today – pattern for this week really. Why did I get a puppy at a time when I was so busy? Stupid.

David generally coped well with Gus but they had one accident in the sitting room.

Gus seemed less bothered by the dustette today.

We let Gus meet an adult male friend at the door on his own four paws for the first time (previously we've always carried him) and he rushed up to say hello. I'm very pleased with his people socialisation so far.

Gus is learning some basic training well. He will sit, down, stand, recall and retrieve when asked reasonably reliably. We will start work on wait soon. Anything to keep his little mind busy and stop him chewing stuff (and us) and getting himself into trouble.

MET: Adult male friend; Tesco delivery driver

EXPERIENCED: Me being out; Dustette

Day 13: 18/9/12

Very much the same as yesterday but without new people or things to see!

Gus and I walked around the garden this morning. I will have to work on training walking nicely on lead some more methinks, because he kept trying to pull and was not really interested in treats. He just wanted to get to the multitude of sniffs in our garden. Well, it's all still so new for him I suppose.

I am now away to England for work from early tomorrow morning to late Thursday night, so I hope everyone will cope.

MET: No one new

EXPERIENCED: Nothing new today

(**Day 14 and Day 15** - no diary entry as I was away. No problems reported by the family.)

Becoming Braver: The Third Week

Day 16: 21/9/12– 10 weeks old

I'm feeling a bit guilty though that I don't have time to focus on Gus as much as I would like to.

How can Gus be ten weeks old already? Where does time go? Though it also feels like he's been here for ages, too. Odd thing, time.

Generally things went well while I was away. There were no major problems or accidents.

David found that cuddling Gus helped him settle and stopped him biting so much. Tonight I noticed that when Gus got tired he asked to be picked up then fell asleep in my arms.

Gus has been trying hard to get up on the chairs today – it won't be long before he can. We'll need to decide whether we want him on the furniture or not and agree the house rules.

I spent today writing up my reports, so I didn't have much time for anything else. Gus settled well on the floor near me in the study, munching his chews and toys. Helpful puppy.

MET: Postman

EXPERIENCED: Dustette and hoover – getting better with both

LESSONS I LEARNED: Looking back, I wish I had had more time to focus on Gus. Running my dog business and doing consultancy work didn't leave much free time. But it's real life. We all muddle along most of the time rather than planning things properly, At least, I do.

By the way, what the house rules are really doesn't matter. Whether the puppy or dog is allowed on furniture or in the bedrooms isn't important. It's your choice. But what IS important is that everyone in the family must be consistent with whatever rules you choose.

Day 17: 22/9/12

Another busy training Saturday.

Gus came out and joined in two of the three dog classes and was very good in each. It's difficult teaching a class and watching him at the same time though.

He learnt to 'leave' with food yesterday evening - I needed to do that following the kebab and chips debacle - and he showed off how well he could do it today.

He's also starting to learn 'wait'. He learns fast. He will retrieve but it is not a very strong urge as yet, which surprises me given his breed.

I took him (driven then carried) to our tennis club at Cloughey at lunchtime. He met loads of children and he just loved it. Though he was tired afterwards. He coped really well with the screaming and shouting they did.

We just messed around together this evening. Gus is biting much less now and even when he does use his little sharp teeth it is far more gentle than it was.

Off to bed, still in his crate by my bed. He sleeps very well every night for usually around 7 hours, which is unusual at this age. But it's wonderful for me!

MET: Lots of children aged 7-17; class dogs and owners

EXPERIENCED: Dog classes, and working in one; Tennis courts and play

Day 18: 23/9/12

Sunday is not a rest day for Gus and I.

We had a very social day today.

Today Gus came to agility class. I got particularly annoyed by him whining and barking when I tied him up whilst I got the agility equipment out. He has hated being restrained or tied up ever since we got him. I must do some training on that. I think he just wants to be involved with everything and hates being prevented from doing what he wants. He's such a nosey puppy.

Gus met two new dogs. One dog was a small springer cross not much bigger than Gus and Gus yapped and yapped at him to try and induce play. It was a bit annoying when I was trying to teach. It all got a bit fraught. Eventually the springer cross got fed up with him and lunged at him. Gus was frightened. He yelped and ran straight to me. I was talking with another client so I just ignored him because I was a bit irritated with him and I didn't want to be interrupted. But at least he settled down a bit after that incident.

I definitely need some earplugs. Gus barks far

too much, at anything and everything.

He's growing so quickly - he's double the weight he was when we first got him and he's grown half as tall again.

Quite a shock this evening - Gus managed to jump up onto my knee. I'm not sure which of us was more surprised! He's been trying for some time but this was his first success. He snuggled down and slept.

Lovely cuddles.

MET: 2 new dogs and owners

EXPERIENCED: Agility class again

LESSONS I LEARNED: I really should have trained Gus to be happy and quiet being tied up from the start. But I never did. To this day he still dislikes it and barks. I didn't handle the incident with the springer cross well. I should have picked Gus up when he ran to me. At this vital stage of his life he needed to know I would always have his back, that he could always come to me if he needed help and that I would respond. I still mourn missing that opportunity at that key moment.

Day 19: 24/9/12

I've been quite irritated by Gus this weekend. The sparkle and fun of a new puppy seems to be going. Probably a culmination of me being so busy, getting behind on my consultancy work, getting frustrated by the constant taking him outside, and constantly stopping him biting and chewing, and it's just feeling too much at the moment.

Frustrating day today. It rained all day and Gus was reluctant to go outside for his pees and poos (don't blame him!). We both got soggy. And wet dog is one of those smells that pervades the whole house...

I did lots of cleaning this morning including cleaning upstairs. Gus tiddled on David's study sheepskin rug when I was distracted. I'm annoyed - it's the rug he poo'd on last week and it's really difficult to clean.

Gus copes relatively OK with the hoover and dustette now. He's still wary of their loud noises, and keeps his distance. But today he decided a fun game was to chase and bite at the brush I was using, so I had to teach him not to do that.

Gus became very hyper again this afternoon. We

are starting to think that the current Jolleyes puppy food may be too high in protein so we've gone back to mixing it half and half with the Burns. I'll keep monitoring this. Of course, it may just be his character - crazy, hyper, bitey puppy.

Tonight I moved the crate from beside my bed to the opposite end of the bedroom. Delighted to say he was happy to go in and he settled down straight away. No more falling over the crate if I have to get up in the night. Bliss.

MET: No one new today

EXPERIENCED: Cleaning - hoover, brush, dustette

LESSONS I LEARNED: The fun of having a new puppy does start to wane after the first couple of weeks. I should have asked for more help from my family, but they were happy to leave most of the work to me, of course, and I'm not good at asking for help from people. Something for me to work on!

Day 20: 25/9/12

Today we had a better day all round.

Gus had a tiddle on David's watch this evening on the floor in the kitchen, but he was clean in the house otherwise.

Gus did really well with some formal(ish!) training on sit, down, stand and wait. He is getting really good at responding quickly. His attention and focus in training is great – and he gets lots of rewards, of course.

Mum and dad called in and Gus greeted them very enthusiastically. He ended up sitting on dad's knee for a cuddle. It was great to see dad's face. Both of them loved it.

The mouthing/biting is getting less, at least most of the time - though he has his moments, especially during the zoomies.

He's growing up.

MET: Mum and dad

EXPERIENCED: Nothing new

Day 21: 26/9/12

Gus was sick at 5.30 this morning – mainly bits of bark.

It's becoming a habit for him to eat bits of the bark mulch from the flowerbeds when we're out on our toilet excursions. So I'm trying to remember to take some bits of kibble out to use as an immediate reward when he toilets. I hope that will keep him more focussed on me and his treats rather than thinking about eating the bark. I hate cleaning up sick as much as I hate cleaning up pee and poo.

Took him for his second vaccination and microchipping at lunchtime. He was a little nervous in the waiting room (odd smells and I was nervous too) but after a slightly wary initial sniff, he cuddled up to the vet. He never even noticed his vaccination or chipping as I made sure he had his nose firmly fixed in his lunchtime meal for each – even though the chipping site bled a little. I was a bit annoyed about that. Clumsy vet?

He saw some cows in the field by our lane today as we drove past – he found them a bit scary and barked at them.

This afternoon he met two more of my adult friends. He behaved very well while they were round.

Gus had a new experience this evening. I took him along (in the car then carried) to the doggy dancing class. He was very good – he did some nice puppy heelwork. He is now shattered.

Hopefully he will still be tired tomorrow when David has him all day as I'm off to England again.

MET: Two adult females; vet; cows

EXPERIENCED: Doggy dancing and upstairs room; Vet waiting room and surgery

(**Day 22** - no diary record as I was away again)

New Things Everywhere: The Fourth Week

(Day 23: 28/9/12 - 11 weeks old - No diary record, I was still away)

Day 24: 29/9/12

Dog training class day again. Lots of activity!

Gus came out to training classes with me. He was able to show off his reasonable basic obedience. Proud mummy! I taught him 'go to bed' as part of the class. He really does pick things up quickly. He was generally good with all the other dogs and people he met. It was a busy morning.

I noticed he was unsettled with all the cars moving about as people came and went from the classes. I must make sure to teach him to ignore cars. I don't want him to become a car chaser, as so many collies are.

Gus slept all afternoon. All this socialising tires a pup out.

I am looking forward to Monday when he can

finally go out and about, as his vaccinations will have kicked in properly.

MET: Dog class people and dogs

EXPERIENCED: Cars moving about the driveway

LESSONS I LEARNED: Collies are chasers of moving things by nature, which is why so many get obsessed by chasing tennis balls. It's fascinating to watch for your puppy starting to show his breed characteristics - knowing what these are and spotting early signs that might lead to poor behaviour later on can really help you stop them becoming a problem.

(**Day 25:** no diary record - I was too busy writing up reports from England.)

Day 26: 1/10/12

Red letter day. Gus was allowed out for the first time on his own four paws today. I'm glad. He's getting too big and heavy to carry for much longer.

Gus came down to Corrog wood with us in the car – he drooled a bit but he wasn't sick. We've put him on a rug on the back seat now and we'll gradually move him into the boot. Small steps. I'm sitting with him.

He was slightly wary of life at ground level, and our walk was very stop-start, unsurprisingly, but he pottered about in the wood and enjoyed the sniffs.

Because Gus had shown at the weekend that he was unsettled with cars moving, we sat for a while and watched several cars go by. He was OK, though not entirely happy. I'm not sure if he is reacting to the noise, or the movement, or both. Another car drew up at the wood car park beside us and he happily met the new people who got out.

On the way back home in the car he was sick, unfortunately. We need to do lots of tiny journeys to try and help him get over his car sickness.

Gus and I got out of the car at the top of our lane and walked back down. He saw a horse for the first time (scary – he growled and barked initially but then settled) and then he saw the cows a bit closer than before (just looked).

What a lot of experiences for a small puppy.

MET: People out and about; horse; cows

EXPERIENCED: Cars going past; First walk – woodland/grass; Car travel again

Day 27: 2/10/12

Second walk out. It's lovely to finally be able to go out and about with him now.

Gus came in the car into Kircubbin then we walked up and down the main street. Gus was fine in the car on his backseat rug for this short journey, although he was not keen to go near the car at first, possibly because David had the engine running. Too impatient, my husband.

Gus was a bit wary of noisy traffic, especially large lorries and buses, but I praised and treated all calm behaviour and he mainly just sat and watched things go by. So much to learn.

He was very keen to meet children in buggies and strollers and he saw lots of different people, some of whom said hello and some of whom ignored him. He thinks all people are great, which I am delighted about.

We went into the pet shop where he discovered the smelly delights of pigs ears. I bought him one – and I had a small growl when I took it away from him. So back at the car (which he got in without problem), I gave him the ear and practised taking it away then giving it straight back with no problems. I don't want him to guard things from me.

Gus was very tired this evening - all those new experiences have taken it out of him.

MET: People out and about; pet shop owner

EXPERIENCED: Traffic going past; Busy village street; Toddlers/babies in strollers

---

LESSONS I LEARNED: Patience is essential with puppies. I'd forgotten that puppies don't actually walk much. They'll often sit and refuse to move, usually because they need time to make sense of what's going on - all those new things to smell, hear and see. It must be sensory overload a lot of the time. Just wait. They'll walk on in their own time.

Day 28: 3/10/12

Third day out and about.

Today we went to Cloughey and walked along the warren and went on the beach. Gus is travelling better now. He sits on a towel on the split back seat/boot, though I always sit on the back seat with him. No sickness today but he still drooled a bit.

Gus jumped at the scary waves crashing onto the shore (more noisy things), but he got used to them fairly quickly. He didn't want to go in the water though. Don't blame him - the Irish Sea is very cold.

He is still showing some wariness with traffic. Cars at Cloughey go past quicker than in Kircubbin, so we spent twenty minutes just hanging around in the car park so we were not too close to the road. He was a bit scared by the traffic going past, but coped better the longer we stayed there. He heard cars hooting their horns too, another new sound.

The children were out playing in the playground at the primary school so Gus and I went over to see them. They were screaming and shouting and they descended on him en masse - and he just loved it! He really is a people dog. Great session for his socialisation.

He was tired afterwards – so many new things.

MET: Children in school

EXPERIENCED: Beach and shore; Traffic; car travel

Day 29: 4/10/12

Gus has been with us for four weeks now and is a major part of our lives.

Today was his fourth day out and about.

We went to Ballyhalbert stables, where Gus met Tricia's horse, Monty, for the first time. They were both quite wary of each other. I'm not surprised. Just Monty's head is twice as big as Gus!

Gus 'helped' us pull the ragwort and ferns from Monty's field and move some of the many stones. He had great fun bouncing about but it's very distracting - I wanted to watch him and kept stopping my weeding to the frustration of daughter. The field backs onto the road, and it helped that plenty of traffic went past whilst we were there. Gus didn't react much at all.

Gus is understandably quite wary of horses at the moment – after all they are very big to a small pup. There was quite a bit of building work going on at the stables, so there were scary cement mixers, diggers and tractors to get used to as well. But there were a lot of people around too.

So Gus had quite a conundrum. Should he

ignore the scary stuff to say hello to wonderful people or not? Usually the people win, which is good.

My friend came round later on and we went outside to say goodbye. Gus was not bothered by her starting her car and driving off, so that is an improvement.

Gus met the lawnmower again, which was sort of OK, but the strimmer is very scary. He ran away.

It's amazing how many different things there are in this world to see and hear. You don't notice until you have a puppy who has to get used to it all.

MET: Monty and other horses; New people at stable; adult female again

EXPERIENCED: Horses and stable area; Lawnmower and strimmer; Traffic

---

LESSONS I LEARNED: Taking your puppy with you wherever you go is great for his socialisation. But it's so easy to overwhelm him. Trying to remember to take things slowly, and especially to give him enough time to cope, can be really hard.

A Bad Experience: The Fifth Week

Day 30: 5/10/12 – 12 weeks old

Horrendous day today.

We drove to the vets to get more wormer today. Gus weighs 8.6Kg now - getting huge. The vet surgery was still shut for lunch, so Gus and I walked from there to the top of Manse Road. It's a country lane, only just wide enough for two vehicles to pass and with no pavement.

It was a short but difficult walk as Gus had some bad experiences.

Unfortunately we met a large bus within the first 5 seconds, then a large tractor and noisy trailer 20 seconds later. Both times Gus shot to the hedge and tried to hide in it. I had to crawl halfway into the hedge to get him out again. It was not a good experience for either of us.

We found a small lay-by area. At this short distance from the road he sat or lay down when cars went past but most times he would not take a treat, showing he was significantly stressed by it all. We will have to do LOTS of training on traffic and noise before walking him along a similar road again. David calls Gus a real traffic wuss, but he really is scared of the noise and speed of traffic.

But back at the vets finally, he met some new people and relaxed a bit.

NOT a good day. Sometimes you do things with the best of intentions and life happens to upset your plans.

MET: New people

EXPERIENCED: Vets with no intervention; Country road and traffic; Worming

LESSONS I LEARNED: With hindsight, taking him along a narrow country lane was perhaps not the best idea, give his wariness of traffic which I knew about, but we were unlucky to meet so much traffic. Sod's law. I should have checked the vet's opening hours too, of course.

Reading this back now, and with the huge benefit of hindsight, I really should have taken him out to see traffic again the next day, in a quiet place of course. Inadvertently I gave him time to internalise the bad experience he'd had. As you will see later on, it took some time to make sure he had some good experiences to counter this bad one.

Day 31: 6/10/12

Gus come out to help with the hens without me using his lead for the first time and he behaved well, just pottering around near me.

He came out to the training class at first but he was just mad today. He would not listen to me at all and he just wanted to sniff around, all the time, so he went back inside with Tricia instead. None of the dogs in any class worked well today – sometimes I think the atmospheric conditions, or air pressure, or something just gets to them. Who knows.

Gus was a pain all afternoon for Tricia. He got into all sorts of mischief, stealing things to get her to chase him and biting a lot again. Tricia's covered in scratches and bruises now. But he settled down later on and was really very good, except for his usual mad half hour just after tea.

He's certainly finding his feet and developing some independence.

MET: Classes – people and dogs

EXPERIENCED: Being out in garden off lead

Day 32: 7/10/12

Gus came out to the arena to play while we set up for agility class.

He tried the weave (gently!) a couple of times and generally behaved very well.

I put him back in the courtyard whilst people were here, but he howled at the back gate for ages. So I let him out to meet people at the end. He's developing quite a character.

Then this afternoon we all went to mum and dad's for tea. Gus stayed on lead in their house - I was too worried that he might sneak off to pee or poo somewhere, or start chewing some precious chair leg, to risk letting him have free run of the place. But he behaved beautifully. No accidents, no biting, no chewing. Well done him.

Apart from the vets, that's the first time he's been in another house or building.

MET: Agility people and dogs

EXPERIENCED: New house and garden

LESSONS I LEARNED: I was sensible to keep him on lead in a new house. Even if your puppy has caught onto the fact you don't want them peeing and pooing in your house they don't inherently understand that they shouldn't pee and poo in anyone else's house either until you've trained that too.

Day 33-34: 8-9/10/12

Two days visiting different places.

Gus had his second beach trip, to Ballywalter beach and promenade yesterday. Today we went to Kircubbin seafront, walking around the estate and back to the car park.

Gus is still nervous of traffic, sitting to watch it pass, but there are definite signs of improvement and I think he is coping OK. He likes the beach but shows no sign of wanting to go into the sea.

At Ballywalter he was mobbed by three young children but behaved very well, wagging his tail and enjoying the petting. He travelled to and from Kircubbin in the boot of the Freelander and he was fine as long as I was in the back seat.

He did a very odd thing yesterday. He barked and jumped around my feet as I was walking on the beach, trying to bite at the tiny bits of sand I kicked up. Odd, but quite cute.

MET: People passing him, some greeting, some not; other dogs; Young children (4-7 years)

EXPERIENCED: Ballywalter beach and seafront; walking round streets in Kircubbin

LESSONS I LEARNED: The odd bouncing round my feet, pouncing on the bits of sand is something that has continued. I'm sure it's a manifestation of his collie instincts to herd and chase moving things, but certainly I've not come across it in any other dog before or since. Just shows Gus is unique - in so many ways!

Day 36: 11/10/12

Nasty weather today – it poured down all day.

Gus walked from the far car park in Ballywalter back to the nearer one along the beach and seafront promenade – and got absolutely soaked. The traffic made hissing noises in the rain which was a bit scary for Gus. He is coping better every day, though he's still a bit wary of all traffic, especially lorries and tractors.

We practised walking nicely to heel using homemade liver cake as the reward which was a big success.

Gus and I went up to see the horses at the stables again. But Monty snorted directly in Gus's face, which frightened him. That made Gus start barking at Monty. I swear Monty did a Muttley-type snigger.

Naughty Monty.

MET: Nothing much – too wet!

EXPERIENCED: Ballywalter promenade and seafront

LESSONS I LEARNED: Gus's reaction to the different noises traffic makes in the rain compared to dry weather should not really have surprised me. It was different, which is why it is so important to make sure your puppy has as many opportunities as possible to see, sniff, hear and meet new things every single day.

Growing in Confidence: The Sixth Week

Day 37: 12/10/12– 13 weeks old

I was panicking today.

Gus seems really big for his age.

I calculated Gus's likely eventual height using an online app. Luckily the answer came out as average for his breed so that's a relief. It is ridiculous how quickly puppies grow though.

Gus came out to help us stack the new logs today, which was the cause of great excitement. The big, noisy delivery lorry made him bark at first. Then we started unloading the logs. Gus raced around the courtyard getting more and more hyper, which led to him tearing chunks out of a plant. So he had to go on a lead and be tied up out of harms way.

When we all came back inside he fell asleep immediately. Overtiredness is definitely a cause of him behaving badly.

Gus is getting a lot braver now and is confident enough to go and explore on his own. This afternoon, having run out to say hello to our postman, he then followed the van back down the drive a little way.

I do hope this is not a first sign of car chasing.

MET: New Postman

EXPERIENCED: Trailer of logs; Stacking logs

LESSONS I LEARNED: Too much stimulation and too many new things happening together can overtire your young puppy. And just as with toddlers, overtiredness can cause bad behaviour.

Days 38-39: 13-14/10/12

Gus had several new experiences this weekend.

We went to mum and dad's house to move some cut gorse with our big trailer. Gus travelled in the boot and I sat in the front seat for the first time.

Gus seemed most affronted that we were so closely followed by a big blue trailer and he barked at it for a while. But he gave up when it didn't go away.

He was very good while we loaded the trailer. Then we took everything to the dump, where there were even more new smells, noises and sights for Gus to see. Going back to mum and dad's, we then stayed for lunch. I let Gus off lead in the house, but he was tired so he stayed close to us.

This afternoon I ran a flyball training session, so Gus came out to meet various people and dogs.

Such a busy day - he was so tired that he slept all Saturday evening. He's sleeping well at nights now too, sleeping for 7-8 hours with no waking up needing to potty. He seems to have a cast iron bladder!

On Sunday we took him to Cloughey again and had a good walk around the beach and warren. Then we sat and watched traffic. He managed a short walk along the pavement near the tennis courts too, which is a big step forward as previously we have only been on the far side of the car park. Cars don't seem to worry Gus much now, thanks to all our practice. He generally ignores cars passing, but he is still wary of noisy lorries and tractors.

Gus stood by the courts and watched two boys playing tennis quite happily. No sign of him wanting to chase tennis balls - yet!

All in all, a good weekend.

MET: Tennis players; Pavement walk at Cloughey

EXPERIENCED: Trailer; travelling in boot of car; dump

Day 40: 15/10/12

Another red letter day.

Gus finally managed to get downstairs on his own!

We've had to carry him down until now. (He's still in his crate in our bedroom at nights). I'm really glad because he's so big and heavy now I was finding carrying him downstairs quite difficult.

Gus came on the outing to mum and dad's again to move the last of the gorse. That big blue trailer followed us again and Gus barked at it for a short while at first.

Gus is now keen to get into the car and seems to have got over any car sickness, thank goodness.

This afternoon Gus had his first experience being in the boot of the Golf with me driving instead of being a passenger on the back seat. I'm delighted to say Gus coped really well and didn't seem bothered that I was not as close to him as before.

We went to Cloughey for a walk on the warren again and had yet more practice being near traffic. He is learning to cope better and better each day.

Practice will make perfect!

MET: People out and about

EXPERIENCED: Trailer again; alone in boot of Golf with me driving

LESSONS I LEARNED: It took until we had had Gus for nearly six weeks for him to be able to come downstairs on his own. Our stairs are steep and turn a sharp corner. He would probably have learned to manage them himself earlier if we had flatter, straight stairs. It also took five or six weeks for him to get over his initial car sickness, which isn't too bad. One of our previous dogs took six months to stop being sick in the car.

(Day 41: No diary entry)

Day 42: 17/10/12

Very cold and wet day.

We decided to go out in the car. Gus is now keen to come out in the car(s), jumping at the boot to try to get in. Will need to train good car manners. Yet another thing to add to my list!

Horrid weather today and because I didn't want to get too wet, Gus went in the boot and I drove him up to the stables to see horses and people again. He also saw calves and kittens, so we had some good socialisation opportunities.

Gus is still barking at horses and finds them scary (I blame Monty), so we need to continue to help him learn to be calmer near horses.

Gus was a real pain with stealing stuff this evening. Every time I took off my slippers he tried to chew one and/or run off with it. After the third time, I decided to do some training on this. I left my slipper on the floor then when he went to take/chew it, I called him to me and rewarded him with a treat instead.

But he quickly got bored of that game and wandered off in search of new trouble.

MET: People out and about; horses, calves and

kittens

EXPERIENCED: Alone in boot of Golf with me driving again

Day 43: 18/10/12

Better day weather wise.

I took Gus to Ballywalter. We walked down behind the shops then back along the main street. He is still wary of traffic (though coping much better) but a couple of people stopped to say hello which he loved.

Then we went down onto the beach where he experienced a pack of small dogs barking at him (scary) as well as meeting a fairly friendly dog. I'm still having to work hard at training him to walk nicely on lead. He's starting to show more interest in chasing a ball though, which I'm pleased about.

Annoyingly, we had a poo accident tonight – the first accident, pee or poo, for ages. I knew he needed a poo and I had taken him outside three times. But of course as soon as I was distracted for a moment it happened.

I was cross with him, even though I knew I shouldn't be. But I'm only human.

MET: People out and about

EXPERIENCED: Walking in street – people, traffic etc.

LESSONS I LEARNED: House training had been going well. Being human I had started to relax my guard a bit, hence the accident. The lesson was to keep up the hawk-like surveillance until your pup has been clean and dry in the house for at least three weeks.

Developing Habits: The Seventh Week

Day 44: 19/10/12– 14 weeks old

My bundle of fluff is getting bigger.

Gus is growing up rapidly.

He took himself off for a poo this morning after we fed and cleaned out the hens. Perhaps my annoyance last night had an effect.

I had a dog visit as well as new training classes today, then I went to a Quiz in Portaferry with mum, so David had Gus from lunchtime onwards.

They went out in his car, then for a short walk.

No problems reported.

MET: People out and about

EXPERIENCED: Alone in boot of Freelander with David driving

Day 45-48: 20-23/10/12

We've only got around 2 more weeks of the key socialisation period left now, so I am doing a quick review of what Gus still needs to see, hear or meet.

<u>Going well</u>

- He is great with people of all ages, happy to meet them and say hello. He hasn't met many babies and toddlers, but we see them regularly in Kircubbin and he's been fine with the ones he has met and heard. I'm particularly pleased that he greets men as happily as women.

- He's met quite a few dogs and, apart from sometimes a little initial uncertainty especially with bigger dogs, he is happy to say hello and interact.

- He is fascinated by hens, happy with sheep, but slightly fearful of cows and of horses. It didn't help that Monty snorted at him when we were at the stables recently. Poor Gus and naughty Monty.

- He is generally happy in the house but some things still worry and scare him. He copes with the dustette but keeps away from the hoover. I'm actually OK about that - better he goes off to another room and keeps out of the way than he attacks it.

- He seems happy with all the other kitchen equipment like the dishwasher, washing machine and tumble dryer. He doesn't try to get in the bins and is polite around food. We've also taught him to ignore brushes now after his initial attack on one.

- He seems happy with most places we go and he's happy to walk on different surfaces, though he is a bit wary of metal gratings and covers.

Things to improve

- He seems scared of loud noises and still doesn't like large, heavy traffic or even lots of cars when it's busy. This seems to be fairly speed dependent - slow cars don't bother him, but cars going at any speed do. Mostly it's lorries and tractors he reacts to. Keeping a good distance is crucial.

- He also reacts (barks) to some odd noises such as my computer mouse wheel and squishy chairs that make a sighing noise when you sit on them (like my study chair).

- He barks when scared/nervous of something or if something surprises him. I suspect he will be a bit of a barky dog.

- He seems fine in the car now and travels well in the boot with no sign of drooling or sickness.

- He has shown some possible tendency to chase cars so we will need to be careful about this.

<u>Other notes</u>

- No accidents all this week.

- Gus is starting to run to us then run towards the door to tell us when he wants to go out. He's also starting to understand to pee on cue (I use "tiddles"). He's settled down into a regular routine of two poos a day, morning and evening. He's eating well but the poos are sometimes a bit soft. I may think about changing his food to see if that helps.

- We go out for regular walks every day, but we are making sure not to over exercise him. We are sticking to the recommended five minutes per month of life twice each day, so we currently walk for about 30-40 minutes in total each day. He gets lots of off lead running about on beaches, at Kearney and at home too. Walking on lead nicely is a work in progress.

Days 49-50: 24-25/10/12

I was so proud of Gus yesterday.

We went to Keaney for our walk. Gus was off lead pottering about and sniffing in the grassy hillocks, when a family appeared, two adults and two young children. Before I realised what was happening, both the children ran up to Gus and flung their arms around him while their parents looked on indulgently. I'm delighted to report that Gus, after an initial startled look, tolerated the invasion of his personal space very well and succumbed to the hugs and attention.

But why do people allow their children to run up to pet a strange dog? I didn't know them and they didn't know me or Gus. Even worse, the children threw their arms around him and hugged him. Some dogs would have objected strongly to that, with good reason. But of course if anything had happened and Gus had reacted and snapped or bitten, the parents (and our law) would have seen him as being in the wrong. Unfair to dogs.

Today Gus surprised me by jumping up at dad. He hasn't done that before, but I shouldn't really have been surprised. It's a very natural thing for dogs to do when greeting someone. So we are now training him to sit to say hello. Mum is great at helping train him, dad not so much. Dad doesn't really like dogs and he gets cross very quickly if Gus does something he doesn't want. Typical that Gus chose dad to jump up at!

He has barked once or twice today at things (cars, people etc.) going past outside. Collie behaviour? Or is he just a dog who reacts to things very easily? I suspect the latter and I think he's going to be a barky dog.

Settling Down: The Eighth and Ninth Weeks

Day 51: 26/10/12– 15 weeks old

Gus has been with us nearly half his whole life now.

We have settled into a routine and there is not so much new to put into these diary records so they are dropping off a bit, despite my good intentions.

Gus is getting good at all basic cues (sit, down, come, wait) and responds well with food treats, though not always as well without.

I was so proud of him today. He behaved brilliantly at mum and dad's, peeing on cue prior to going into the house, then generally being really good while we were there.

He is great in the car, generally very quiet (except when we pull the scary big blue trailer) and he waits quietly in the car if we go into a shop. We have not left him for long alone in the car, but certainly a few minutes are fine.

I'm really busy with work in England again this week so David has responsibility for him most days and also has the walking duties.

Days 52-54: 27/10/12 - 29/10/12

Another good few days.

No accidents at all in the house and Gus is regularly asking to go out when he needs to.

David reported no problems on walks and Gus is generally walking nicely on lead. I have noticed that he coughs occasionally especially when he pulls a bit and I'm wondering if he has a sensitive larynx? Just like me hating polo necks. I might think about getting him a harness instead to see if that helps.

He's also started to bite a bit more again and I had to stop him chewing a chair leg yesterday- is he starting to teethe possibly?

To: 2/11/12– 16 weeks old

Gus is getting really grown up now! He did really well at our training class this week to the chagrin of others (I was a proud mum). We didn't run agility - it was too wet.

But we had a difficult time when I had a client here.

Gus knew I was outside and drove David mad with his howling and scraping at doors. He broke my crown Derby saucer when he jumped up on the windowsill. I had made a note to do some training on separations after he'd had that paddy a week or so ago when I left him in the courtyard, but I haven't done nearly enough (or much at all if we're honest. Where does time go? Must try and do more training.)

Gus is also not always doing as he's told, especially when he's over excited. For example: not always sitting when visitors come. We will need to practice this more, especially as he is now getting more confident and moving rapidly towards adolescence.

He generally walks well on lead now. He still needs occasional reminders not to pull, but he's not too bad.

Gus is still wary of traffic but there are definite signs of improvement. We've done lots of work at Cloughey near to, but not too close to, the road. That car park area is ideal for this practice as there is loads of room to move further away from traffic if Gus gets a bit stressed.

Gus had two bad experiences with other dogs on walks this week. The first was when an old female collie sniffed him up his bottom too long and he surprised me by snarling and then he snapped at her. (I should have interrupted the sniffing earlier.) The other one happened today on our walk where Gus yelped when a big chocolate lab ran up very rudely and bowled him over. Annoying, but I think it was surprise more than hurt; I can't find any injury and Gus seems fine now.

Toilet training is no problem now – he asks to go out around every three or so hours. We've just reached the magic three-weeks-with-no-accidents, so this week we'll start letting him out on his own to toilet. Selfishly, I'm glad. It's getting far too cold and wet to be standing out with him.

We wormed him again today – his next worming will be due at nine months old.

Gus is hardly biting us at all now, but I need to watch him closely as he will chew the fixtures and fittings given a chance. We keep several different chew toys handy at all times.

Summary of socialisation

In general I feel we have done well and covered most things. It's really helped to keep this diary so I could keep track of the number and types of people he met, even though I've let accurate diary records lapse a bit lately. I must develop a good checklist then I can share it with clients too.

From now on its all about continuing the good work and watching for any issues.

LESSONS I LEARNED: I did produce a socialisation checklist. Find out how to get hold of a copy in the Next Steps section at the end of this book.

Growing Up: Month 3

To 9/11/12– 17 weeks old

I feel sad. Gus is growing up and getting gangly. Where has my cute, tiny bundle of fluff gone?

Gus is showing some signs of being worried when he hears dogs bark when out, even if they are some way away. I don't react, instead I jolly him along, but he is still a little stressed when it happens. This started after he had those two bad experiences last week. Must try to find some nice dogs for him to meet.

Gus is definitely reactive to noise – he barks at unusual noises or ones he has not yet got used to, such as the recycling bins being dragged over the gravel, airplanes flying low overhead, tractors or big lorries (he is generally ignoring most cars now).

Gus came on an exciting trip this week. We took him to the centre of Newtownards and he was great. He was so excited to see and try to meet all the new people that he didn't seem to bother about the traffic. He startled at a couple of sudden, loud noises but it was not a big problem. He is more bothered by traffic at quiet spots when it is intermittent, it seems.

Gus humped his bed and a cushion for the first time this week. He's definitely growing up.

He also had a great time pulling the stuffing out of one of his toys. I hadn't the heart to stop him - he was enjoying it too much. Much better doing that than him chewing our furniture.

Interestingly, Gus is showing some odd behaviour in my study. He seems obsessed by the TV stand and Sky box. I'll have to put a guard round it as he bites at the Sky box whenever I use certain craft tools (especially my die cutting machine) and it's getting worse. It's difficult to distract him. He's also showing the same behaviour with the computer base in David's study. I wonder if it's some high-pitched electronic sound that's attracting his attention? I may try switching all the stuff off and see if the behaviour reduces.

LESSONS I LEARNED: I didn't switch the electronic stuff off, neither did I really do anything else. I wish now I had tried harder to interrupt and stop these odd behaviours when I first noticed them.

Puppies learn things so quickly that it is easy for them to develop habits you might not want later on. I didn't even start to try and address this odd barking for another couple of weeks (see week 20), which allowed the behaviour to become a habit. Gus still does some odd barking at the TV stand and Sky box even today.

To 16/11/12– 18 weeks old

Gus is now enjoying all his walks.

Things he still gets scared by: big dogs, small aggressive dogs, and still some (heavy/noisy) traffic. He walks very nicely on lead now most of the time, only pulling very occasionally when he gets excited.

His recall is good, so he is now allowed off lead. Gus comes back every time when called with me, often offering nice off-lead walking by my side too for considerable periods. Those food rewards work well!

Gus loves the beach, enjoys short fetch games with a ball and walks quite well around the local villages. Training is going well and he responds to all the usual basic cues including sit, down, stand, wait/stay, come, walk nicely and leave.

I've got problems with him at tennis club though. Gus lulled me into a false sense of security when we first watched tennis, when he did not react to tennis balls being hit at all. Now he is getting way too excited and aroused by tennis balls being hit when he is close to the courts, so I need to keep him further away. I tried with me playing and him tied up near the courts, but he got very stressed, yapping and barking and he was generally pretty horrid. Given the court's position near a road I cannot let him free off lead there, so I'm not sure if he will ever get to the stage of being able to come with me to tennis or not. We'll need to do much more training on his settling down at a distance from me first.

Our other problem area is in the car. He seems fine when with me in the Golf, but David has reported him barking at other vehicles when he's in the Freelander. It happens when other cars are pulling up alongside, or overtaking, mainly. Do we need to think of using a car crate for Gus?

To 23/11/12– 19 weeks old

Gus continues to progress and develop well, generally.

David is having the odd problem with him not coming back on walks, usually when Gus wants to go and say hello to other people or dogs. I have encouraged David to use treats. Gus comes back for me with no problems at the moment.

Gus seems to be fascinated by small spaniels more than any other breed. I noticed that in training here – he was fixated on trying to play with Daisy, a small springer spaniel, during her one to one sessions. It is starting to become more difficult to keep his attention on me when other dogs and people arrive for training. Though once they are here and he has said hello he settles after a short while and behaves better.

Gus has starting teething now in earnest but he has been good (so far!) about chewing only his chews and toys. We have had only one or two casualties – one branch of the plant in the hallway (a favourite for a surreptitious chew from the start) and the plastic purple flower stems from by the fireplace which we discovered in pieces after breakfast one morning when he'd been suspiciously quiet.

We're still having some problems with Gus barking in the car, but not every time. It seems to be once he starts, he continues, but sometimes he doesn't start. It definitely seems worse in the Freelander. It's only happened once with me when we were in the Golf. That was at dusk and other car headlights started to go on, which I felt was the trigger. He also barks when we tow the trailer, but this usually settles after a short while. It can be wearing though. Not sure what to do about it. Covered crate?

To 30/11/12– 20 weeks old

Gus is getting bolder.

He's now not come back when called twice in the garden, preferring to eat the bird food than respond to my call. We will need to practice recall a lot more.

Gus now has a bed by my desk to try and forestall/distract him from rushing at the TV and barking (see week 17). We are practising Gus going to his bed and staying there, which works fairly well if I have treats available.

He is enjoying his walks with David and he is generally a pleasure to take on walks. One day this week he got frightened by cows charging across a field towards him at Kearney. He shot off with his tail between his legs. David only caught up with him again when they got to Kearney village.

Gus enjoys coming to some training classes. But this week I have struggled more to keep his attention during classes. It may be a combination of his age and my not doing so much training this past two weeks plus he can't do anything much at agility yet of course as he's still too young. We need to do more training (lots more training) in distracting situations.

Gus is great in the house generally. He likes his home comforts, often choosing the settee, though increasingly often he moves to the floor to lie down to snooze. He still enjoys a cuddle, but is not just quite so cuddly as he was initially....sad.

Still some annoying barking in the Freelander. Will look at car crates.

LESSONS I LEARNED: I did a lot of basic training in the house, as you have read, but I didn't do nearly enough training out and about in different places with all sorts of different distractions. I always emphasise with clients how important it is to practice everything your dog knows in as many different places with as many different distractions as possible. But I know from experience now just how difficult it is to follow that advice!

Adolescence Hits: Month 4

To 7/12/12– 21 weeks old

It's feeling like Groundhog Day every day at the moment.

I am still struggling with stopping Gus barking at the TV/Sky box in my study when I make any sort of noise at all. I'm not really sure why he does this and distraction only works intermittently. I'm now wondering if it's an echo or something that he's reacting to because of the bare concrete floor. Or is it just a habit now? I'll see what happens to the behaviour when the new floor is put down, which should be in the next few weeks.

Gus still occasionally steals things and tries to run off with them. He gives things up happily but only when cornered. I need to work harder on teaching him retrieve. My bra and slippers are firm favourites for stealing.

He walks nicely on lead now just about all of the time. David is much happier now both looking after him when I'm out and with walking him.

We are still working on stopping the barking in the car. Interestingly he does not do it much in the Golf – perhaps he can see more from the Freelander? It happens principally when cars come up close behind, or when we are towing the trailer, or when cars pass close at the side when they are overtaking or turning.

I'm struggling to deal with some of these problems. Even though I know all the theory, it can be difficult to put it into practice and especially to find the time to do it. I've got my Kennel Club assessment in January which is taking time to prepare for, never mind getting ready for Christmas and still having a lot of work in England. And I swear Gus is finding things to do that aren't even in the dog training books just to test me. Like barking at planes and barking at the TV/Sky box.

December 2012 – 5 months old

We had an Andrex puppy moment this week.

Gus suddenly appeared backing into the bedroom with toilet paper rolling out behind him! It wasted nearly a whole roll. I did some training on 'leave'ing the toilet rolls...

He is turning out to be a great dog in most ways. Though the barking in my study and the car is still a nuisance and I need to continue trying to stop this.

Gus's general training is coming on well. He did a lovely round in the last training class before the break. I must try to find more time for training him in the New Year. I've been frantically trying to finish knitting a jumper for my dad for Christmas so any spare time this month has been on that rather than Gus. (The jumper did get finished though and dad loved it.)

The Christmas decorations survived better than I expected.

Gus had a good sniff round the tree when I first put it up, but apart from one ornament which seems to have taken his fancy (one I had made), he has left things well alone.

He made me laugh last week though. I set out my musical Christmas toys and played them. He barked wildly at them because he couldn't work them out at all at first, but things are settling down now.

Amazingly he has not bothered trying to get at any of the presents under the tree.

On Christmas Day itself Gus was very good though it may be another year before he really understands presents. Once he'd had his first one (a chew) he settled down with that and was not interested in the others which contained toys.

He was good during Christmas lunch and lay down near the table - mind you I think he was full of turkey skin by then anyway.

David's cousin came over with her 18 month-old labrador, Libby. Gus was fine with the cousin, but Libby was rather a bully with Gus, so I had to intervene a couple of times to stop her pestering him. He just loves the new Kong cuddly toy she brought him.

We are also practising him being calmer when going to other people's houses (especially mum and dad's). He gets very frustrated when kept on lead – tough. He will learn.

Snow Fun: Month 5

January 2013 - 6 months old

Well, one New Year resolution must be to do more training.

I have let it slip a bit recently because I've been so busy with work from England and preparing for my Kennel Club assessment at the end of the month.

Gus and I went up to our training room one very wet day last week, intending to train - only to find puddles of water all over the floor. It had come in under the door we think during the very wet and windy weather over Christmas. David has fiddled with the door trying to stop it happening again and I mopped up – so reduced time for training again….

Gus is going through an odd stage – testing the boundaries a bit methinks (teenage phase starting?) by not coming when we call, instead he stands and looks at us for a bit first as if to say, should I or not….? We will need to do a lot more training on recall.

I find I need to vary the exercises, treats and rewards frequently during a session as Gus quickly gets bored with the same things. Typical adolescent dog.

Key things we need to work on are:

- Quick and immediate response to recall

- Recall from distractions

- Ignoring distractions generally – better focus and self-control

- Reducing nuisance barking – he gets quickly wound up when he hears something outside, barks a lot, then takes a while to settle again. He also barks occasionally in the car when moving, when there is a lot of traffic, or traffic is passing/overtaking. This has not got any better.

20th January

Snow! Gus had his first experience of snow – he went mad charging around. He loved chasing snowballs. Tricia got some great pictures.

26th January

I had my Kennel Club Assessment over the past two days. The assessor came to the house today to quiz me and complete the assessment.

Embarrassingly, as he walked in, Gus came charging in and jumped up at him. Oh, the shame! Luckily Gus behaved well otherwise and I passed at advanced level. A huge relief.

Shan't, Won't: Month 6

February 2013 – 7 months old

Gus is no longer a puppy, but has morphed into a true adolescent.

Most of the time he behaves quite well but sometimes he just does a Kevin, (the Harry Enfield teenager) and says "oh, muuum". I can really see Kevin in the way he looks at me; it's spooky.

Gus's recall still needs work but is generally good. Recall from a distraction can be an issue occasionally but usually he turns on a sixpence and comes straight back, bless him. He is starting to settle down though he still has his mad puppy moments.

I'm finding it difficult to have him with me in training classes as he is too distracted by other dogs. It's annoying as he works exceptionally well on his own. We need LOTS more work with distractions. He's a typical "shan't, won't" adolescent at times.

He barks at lot in the car at other vehicles passing us in heavy traffic or when large vehicles appear, or when cars get too close behind. I now sit in the back to try to keep him calmer and less aroused when I can. It works well but isn't possible every time. So he's still getting (lots of) practice at barking in the car. And practice is making perfect...

We've tried him in a covered crate, but it makes no difference. I suspect this barking may become an ongoing problem. It's difficult because obviously if there's just one person in the car, you can't drive and train him at the same time. I wish now I'd started with a car crate from the beginning and taught him to lie down in it. Possibly a bit late now.

He still shows little interest in tennis balls which is a shame as I really want him to do flyball. Tug is his favourite game.

I'm not going to neuter him yet, despite the vet suggesting it. Gus is still occasionally fearful of things so I want him to get the full benefit of the testosterone. I also want him to be fully grown and developed. I do feel so many dogs are neutered too early nowadays which is not good for their skeletal development.

Gus gave me another new problem this week. He started running up and down the hedge in the arena as cars were coming and going. I hadn't really noticed it until now. But now I'm noticing because he is barking as he runs up and down. I should have nipped it in the bud. I'm worried he could chase cars if he gets the opportunity, so we'll have to be careful.

Adolescence often brings these sorts of problems to the fore. Sigh.

LESSONS I LEARNED: Adolescence is such a trying time for most dog owners. I wish I had thought more about how I wanted Gus to ride in the car right from the start. I had never had a dog who barked in the car before, even though it is quite a common problem, so early on I concentrated on stopping him being sick rather than teaching him how I wanted him to behave in a car. I should have introduced a crate very early on which may well have prevented the problem. Or it may not - give his natural high arousal and reactivity it might not have made any difference. We will never know!

Chaos to Calmish: A puppy diary

Ears Erect!: Month 7

March 2013 – 8 months old

Gus is really growing up now. He has filled out more physically, though his legs are still a bit gangly.

The biggest change is that his ears have become fully erect. They look like satellite dishes. They are huge too. No wonder he reacts to noises - he must be able to hear everything for miles.

We have started going out with the Ballyhalbert walking group every Thursday. It gives Gus lots of socialisation and practice walking with other people, plus Jessie, an elderly Scottie, teaches him manners.

Gus is getting much better with traffic and coped really well with quite heavy and fast traffic when walking along the main road to Greyabbey from Harrisons last week. Though he got a bit stressed on the return walk, as the traffic was coming from directly behind him and he found that more difficult to cope with.

He is getting better in the car and barks less. The main triggers are large tractors, very large lorries (sometimes) and cars passing close (e.g. in dual lane queues). My sitting in the back helps so I will continue with this whenever possible.

His recall is now very good - nearly always.

I had one bad experience at the Floodgates when a spaniel came running up. Gus said hello nicely - but when I walked on and called Gus, expecting him to come with me, I suddenly realised he was not there. He was still playing with the spaniel to that owner's annoyance....oops. Frustrating, as Gus had come each time I called him away from four other dogs on the same walk. Dogs - who'd have 'em?

He's starting to play more and chase a tennis ball, which I'm encouraging.

Crowds and Noise: Month 8

April 2013 – 9 months old

Gus has really left puppyhood behind now.

He is generally doing really well. We have no real problems with traffic now when out walking. But when he's in the car he still barks at certain large vehicles, such as lorries or tractors, or at cars when they are very close behind us, though not all the time.

I may try blocking the car windows to see if that helps, as it is when the vehicles are moving down the side of the car that it generally happens, or if we are overtaken (only happens when David is driving!)

I took him to Mount Stewart Pet Nose Day this month. It's a big event. We were doing a flyball demonstration, there were agility demonstrations, Bernese Mountain dogs pulling carts, a pet dog show and loads of stalls.

The organisers counted 1,109 people and over 2,000 dogs through the gate, so it was very busy.

Gus barked as usual when tied up during our flyball demonstrations. The barking when tied up really needs attention. (I really should have worked on that. I meant to do it…)

But I forgave him as he was SOOO good otherwise. He walked around beautifully, on a loose lead, not reacting to all the odd things such as people dressed as cats, odd noises and smells and dogs charging around doing agility. He wanted to say hello to other dogs but generally desisted on cue.

I was so proud of him.

Fight or flight: Month 9

May 2013 – 10 months old

It feels like Gus has been here forever, now.

In general he's doing very well, but we still have some issues.

Gus's barking in my study now seems just focused on me sitting on my desk chair. It makes a sighing noise when I sit on it and that seems to be the trigger. Oddly enough, he barks briefly when I type at the desk, but he doesn't react to my typing if I'm doing it anywhere else, such as the kitchen. It must be some odd noise or resonance that he's reacting to. I am trying hard to work on stopping this. At least the Sky box doesn't get attacked very often nowadays.

Gus is quite a reactive dog and barks more readily at anything he hears than any other collie we have had. He is very easily aroused and excited.

We are still trying to stop him barking in the car. Our current method involves covering the back side windows in the car with blackout material, which seems to help reduce the barking a bit. On some journeys we have no barking, but sometimes odd things still set him off.

Gus had three bad experiences this month.

The first bad experience was that Gus had a bit of a fight with the labrador who lives at the top of our lane. Now this labrador barks madly at us whenever we walk past - and not in a friendly way - but he usually stays in his own garden. On this day, the dog came through the hedge as we were walking past. He just leapt straight at Gus and there was quite a scuffle. Luckily there didn't seem to be any damage to either dog, but I was really cross it had happened. I will have to pluck up the courage to have a word with the lab's owners and see if they will either keep him in, or put a better fence up.

His second bad experience was in the kitchen. We got a new toaster. The first time we used it Gus was right by it when it pinged. He got a real scare and ran off and he now is scared to go into the kitchen area. This might be a second fear period thing?*

The third (and final) bad experience was that Gus scared himself silly falling down the stairs last week. He was trying to run down too fast and he tumbled head over heels. He didn't seem to have hurt himself, but it shook him up (and me) badly. Since then he has refused to go down stairs himself. We have to carry him and he's now a bit big for me to carry him safely.

We have been doing much more training on attention with distractions around this month and it is helping his focus and general behaviour out and about - which is actually quite good anyway!

He's now getting quite good at fetching a tennis ball, as long as I don't throw it too often. I'm hoping he might become my flyball dog after all.

Must say, apart from his barking and the kitchen scare, we are getting through adolescence with few problems. I hope that statement isn't going to be the kiss of death....

LESSONS I LEARNED: *Dogs have a second fear period anytime between 6 and 11 months old, when they are very susceptible to sudden fears about things they had previously not bothered with. Gus has remained fearful of going into the kitchen area ever since the event with the toaster.

Settling Down: Month 10

June 2013 – 11 months old

Those ears just keep on growing. They really are <u>so</u> big.

Gus is now just about fully grown height wise and he's filling out well.

All in all I'm proud of him. He's generally well behaved, loves all people and is friendly to everyone. I just wish he'd be a bit more cuddly sometimes, but he's a real boy. He tolerates short cuddles and little bits of fuss, but then gets all squirmy and says "Get ooofffff" in a non-verbal, but very obvious sort of way.

We still have some issues:

- Barking in my study and in the car. I can manage it, but I don't think I'll ever stop it completely now. I was over in England for work quite a lot in his first few months and perhaps didn't focus enough on Gus's training and picking up problems early enough.

- David reports that sometimes Gus runs up to people on the beach and jumps around their feet, ready to bite at the bits of sand their feet throw up. I can see that it's scary for people when that happens. I know he's not being aggressive, but they don't. It's something he's done since the very first time we went on the beach. I suppose I should have stopped it then but I thought it was quite cute. We need to keep his attention on other things when on the beach. I have no problem, as I keep him engaged with his ball thrower and training practice, but David goes off into a world of his own sometimes - and Gus is easily bored, so he soon starts looking for ways to entertain himself.

- Running up and down the arena hedge as cars are coming and going has become a habit. It may be too late now to stop this tendency I feel, though I will try. I will just have to manage things better and keep him focused on me - and keep him on lead if necessary.

Following the scuffle with our neighbour's labrador last month, Gus surprised me by running off when we were in the garden one day recently. We found him up the laneway by the hedge where the lab came through. Both dogs were running up and down either side of the hedge - Gus in the lane and the lab in his garden - barking at each other. Not good.

Gus's not-wanting-to-come-downstairs has

turned into not wanting to go upstairs either, so he now sleeps on the sofa in the front room. His choice, even though he has a perfectly good dog bed in the kitchen. But I don't mind that.

He goes up stairs and steps quite happily anywhere else. I think he finds our staircase so difficult because our stairs are very steep and turn a sharp corner. They are also wooden and so a bit slippy.

One bad thing - Gus ran across the northern beach at Ballywalter to chase after a car that was pulling onto the grass last week. I was horrified. Mea culpa - I should have stopped it or prevented it. We will need to be very careful about keeping him on lead near moving cars in future.

But overall, he's turning into a great dog.

One year and counting

July 2013 – 1 year old!

I can't believe where the time has gone. Where did the last 10 months go?

Gus has turned into a great dog (mainly) and he'll get lots of presents next week.

LESSONS I LEARNED

I stopped the diary entries after that last one above. It's interesting looking back. The issues I noted in that first year are still the ones I'm having to manage and deal with. It shows just how much of any dog's traits and character come out and can be seen very early on in their lives.

Gus the dog

Gus is much the same today, at six years old, as he was aged one. Still a high energy, mad, farm collie. He's generally great in the house. But he runs from window to window, often barking, when David's outside working in the garden. He hates being left in the house when someone's outside, but he's fine when we leave him to go out.

I did eventually neuter him, at 13 months. Looking back, I should probably have left it longer than that, until he was 18 months or 2 years old. Or not neutered him at all. He was still showing some nervousness at 13 months old (and still does today, especially to loud noises). Leaving neutering until he was older (or not doing it at all) may have helped him cope better with noises and helped build a bit more confidence, because of the higher levels of testosterone. We will never know.

Gus loves all people and most dogs. Like many adult dogs, he prefers to meet with a few doggy friends and generally ignores other dogs. He loves people and enjoys meeting old friends and new faces.

He is a very strong-willed (bit stubborn) dog and will worry at a problem and keep pestering if he wants something. He's trained us well; he comes and paws at me in the evening when he thinks it's time for his biscuits. He's trained David well, too: Gus stops and lies down if he doesn't want to go somewhere. David either tries to drag him or takes him back to the car and walks on alone. I don't. I use cunning and wait things out, so I don't have much problem with him doing that with me. He walks on after a minute or two.

Day to day life

Annoyingly, Gus has taught himself to open all the doors in the house, inwards as well as outwards. I certainly didn't encourage or train that! But I do secretly admire his persistence and skill. He even managed to open the front door by turning the key. Now we have to keep the front door locked and the key out, or he will let himself out and go up the lane. He goes to where he had the fight with the neighbouring labrador, even though we haven't seen that dog for over a year now. Perhaps he met a sticky end. At least we always know where to find Gus if he ever does get out.

Gus did become obsessed with flyball and we had some great times. But he got himself hugely over-aroused by it, bouncing around like Tigger. He kept getting a low-level hip problem from all the jumping, pulling and charging about. I was thankful when we stopped it last year (2017). We also tried agility for a while but Gus didn't enjoy it and, if truth be told, neither did I.

His training was very interrupted by my health problems too. The long-standing arthritis in my knees was made worse following a car accident in November 2013. I ended up with two knee replacements, in 2014 and 2016. Luckily things are great now, but Gus's training definitely lost out for those crucial early years. But hey, life happens.

Ongoing problems

Gus is still noise sensitive and that has become worse with some things. Looking back in this diary I see I noticed it first as early as day 3. I should have worked far harder on helping him with that. I could have played a scary sounds CD regularly and done lots more training to help him get used to different noises. But the retrospectoscope is a fine thing, of course.

A couple of years ago, people locally started shooting over ground to either side of us. Gus became very fearful of gunshots, diving into the garage to find somewhere to hide. (He's generally OK with those noises when in the house). I'm still working hard on helping him chose a better option than panicking with those sudden, loud noises even today and he can now cope a little better. It's very much work in progress.

Gus got stung by a bee last year and had a full blown panic attack, luckily we were around to help him. But this has developed into a fear of any buzzy things and he will shoot out of a room if there is a loud buzzing noise. I'm working on this, too.

He still won't come upstairs here, though he will walk happily upstairs and steps anywhere else. The only time that is a problem is if there's a thunderstorm during the night and he's unsettled. Then he wants to come up with me when I go to bed. Once or twice he's managed it but it can be a real palaver getting him down again in the mornings - he's too big for me to carry now.

Barking in my study has become a habit in response to two main triggers; me sitting down on my chair, which makes a sighing noise, and when I start typing. But he soon quickly settles down quietly and then I can type away happily.

Gus still barks in the car. He reacts to movement of other cars. I'm pretty sure he would be a bad car chaser if he got the chance - but we are careful never to let him off lead near moving cars. In the car, he never barks when we've parked up, but starts as soon as we start to move. The barking is worst when a car is very close behind us or overtakes us, or when we overtake another car. Interestingly it seems to vary with which model and make of car he's in. Some are definitely worse than others.

We tried lots of things, including a covered crate, a travel crate on the back seat and a dog tunnel. We've found he's better when in the front seat and he's fine if I sit with him on the back seat. I've tried to get him to stay lying down in the car (which stops the barking). But I know I haven't done nearly enough training on it.

Gus will leave the room when we use the hoover but he is not particularly bothered by it - he knows he can just keep away and everything is fine. But he's not been happy to go into the kitchen area ever since his fright with the toaster. I can live with that too.

What I learned

My own development and training has come on a long way since 2012-2013. I'd do quite a lot of things differently now, as you've seen from the 'lessons I learned' notes in this book. In particular I'd pick up much earlier on possible future problems (like barking in the car) and make sure I did something about them proactively rather than only trying to deal with it once it has become a problem.

I know a lot more now. That knowledge is all in my book, *Pesky Puppy to Perfect Pet,* which is a modern puppy bible. It's available via our website and from Amazon in paperback and on Kindle. (The links can be found in the next chapter.)

Gus is not perfect (no dog is) but I understand all his foibles and to me he's my (nearly) Perfect Pet.

Calmish has followed that early chaos.

Carol Clark

September 2018

NEXT STEPS

Wondering what to do next? Here are three things that may help:

1) If you want help with your new puppy or dog, start with my puppy bible: *Pesky Puppy to Perfect Pet.* It's available:

   - from Amazon in paperback
     https://amzn.to/2MDUHTi

   - as a Kindle eBook
     https://amzn.to/2QCTVce

   - or from my website,
     https://downdog.co.uk/Perfect_Pooch_2017

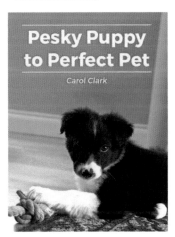

2) Download the Puppy Socialisation Checklist so you know what people, animals, places, situations and experiences your new puppy needs to find out about. It's available from my website, https://downdog.co.uk/Articles There are lots of other free help sheets there too, as well as details of our courses and services. We're planning to add online training courses from Autumn 2018.

3) Sign up for my FREE Ten Training Tips series. Go to https://downdog.co.uk/# pop your details in the sign up boxes and my first tip will wing its way to your inbox as soon as you've pressed submit. You'll also receive my regular emails on a variety of topics, including plenty of hints and tips about training and dog behaviour.

Chaos to Calmish: A puppy diary

Printed in Great Britain
by Amazon

48017720R00083